HOW TO HELP YOUR LOVED ONE OVERCOME DEPRESSION

A FAST SIMPLE SYSTEM TO RELIEVE DISTRESS

Dr James Manning, ClinPsyD
Dr Nicola Ridgeway, ClinPsyD

Published by The West Suffolk CBT Service Limited
Registered office: Angel Corner, 8 Angel Hill,
Bury St Edmunds, Suffolk, IP33 1UZ

How to help your loved one overcome depression
A fast simple system to relieve distress

Dr James Manning, ClinPsyD
Dr Nicola Ridgeway, ClinPsyD

A product of the West Suffolk CBT Service Limited
Angel Corner, 8 Angel Hill,
Bury St Edmunds, Suffolk, IP33 1UZ
United Kingdom

Enquiries 01284 723948

This edition printed 2010
Copyright © 2009 West Suffolk CBT Service Ltd

Published in association with

foulsham
The Oriel, Thames Valley Court, 183-187 Bath Road,
Slough, Berkshire, SL1 4AA, England
Website: www.foulsham.com

ISBN – 978-0-572-03517-4

Printed 2010, Europa

Edited by Jenny Roberts and Steven Bee
Design and layout by Mathew Buch

ABOUT THE AUTHORS

Dr Nicola Ridgeway is a Clinical Psychologist and an accredited cognitive and behaviour therapist. She lectures on cognitive behaviour therapy at the University of Essex, the University of East Anglia and is chairperson of the Eastern Counties branch of the British Association of Behavioural and Cognitive Psychotherapists

Dr James Manning is the Managing Director and founder of the West Suffolk Cognitive Behaviour Therapy Service based in Bury St Edmunds, Suffolk. James has post-graduate qualifications in both Clinical Psychology and Counselling Psychology.

DEDICATION

This book is dedicated to
Christine Ridgeway

ACKNOWLEDGEMENTS

Thank you to all the relatives of the West Suffolk CBT service clients, who have assessed and offered feedback about the advice presented in this book.

Many thanks to all the staff at the West Suffolk CBT Service who helped with the production of this book, Steven Bee, Julia Johnson, Nicola Whittaker, Ann Watkins and Karen Millar.

Thank you to Bilbo who as usual continues to be an inspiration to the West Suffolk CBT Service.

PREFACE

If you live with an individual with depression, this book has been written for you.

Working in clinical practice, Dr Ridgeway and I are regularly contacted by relatives for fast-working advice to help their loved one. What is very clear from these conversations is that relatives often feel powerless as they suffer alongside their son, daughter, husband, wife, partner or parent.

The good news is that if you are living with a relative with depression, you can have a major positive impact on their mood, and you can achieve this quite rapidly by making subtle changes to your behaviour.

"How to help your loved one overcome

depression" covers the major traps that it is possible to fall into when we try to help someone who is depressed. It also includes the most effective practical solutions we have come across in our combined thirty years of clinical experience.

We hope that you find this book helpful.

Best wishes,

Dr James Manning
Managing Director
West Suffolk CBT Service

CONTENTS

INTRODUCTION

Whether you are a wife, husband, son, daughter, sibling, partner or a friend, if you live with someone who is suffering with depression, this book has been written for you.

You can play a big part in helping your loved one to recover by altering your own behaviour. An experience of depression does not occur in isolation and symptoms associated with it are often highly reactive and easily influenced by the behaviours of others.

When we live with someone who is experiencing depression, it may surprise us to hear that we have much more of an impact on their symptoms than either they or we realise. Because of this, it is fundamentally important to understand how our behaviour impacts on them.

THE BASICS

There is a big difference between low mood and depression.

Nearly all of us at some point in our life will experience low mood. Low mood is a normal reaction to loss, set backs and failures that we all face from time to time. For most of us, our low mood passes relatively quickly and causes little disruption to our lives.

Depression, on the other hand, is a problem that hangs on for longer periods of time, often causing much more disruption to our lives. Individuals who experience depression have low mood, but are also likely to experience problems with their concentration, memory, sleep, appetite, motivation, energy, libido, and way of thinking.

Depression continues to be a widely misunderstood problem.

Ironically, although depression is very common in our society (during our lives at least one in four of us will experience a significant period of depression), it is still clouded by misunderstanding. Depression often does not make sense to those who have never experienced it. This lack of understanding can often leave individuals who experience depression feeling even worse about themselves.

Depression is like a trap from which it's hard to escape.

For those who experience depression, it can feel like a trap in which the more effort that is used trying to escape from it, the more stuck a person tends to feel. It's not dissimilar to falling into quicksand. Struggling doesn't work, and the strategy that is needed to get out (being still) feels counter-intuitive.

Is positive intention enough?

Our natural instinct when we see someone we love suffering is to try to help. The way we attempt to help someone with depression is very important, because many behaviours – even if carried out with the best intentions – can be harmful, contributing to mood deterioration. When this occurs, we can end up feeling just as helpless as our loved one does.

In the sections that follow, some of the common traps that we all fall into from time to time are described. Then solutions are offered. Ideally, you will think about these solutions, try them out, and then assess for yourself whether or not they work for you and your loved one.

TRAPS

OVERVIEW

WHEN SOMEONE CLOSE TO US
IS SUFFERING WITH DEPRESSION,
WE CAN ENGAGE IN BEHAVIOURS
WHICH, DESPITE OUR MOST POSITIVE
INTENTIONS, CAN END UP WITH US
MAKING THE SITUATION WORSE.

In this section, our straight-to-the-point Cognitive Behaviour Therapist illustrates some of the most common traps that we may fall into when we try to help others who are depressed.

If you find yourself identifying with the traps outlined, it is likely that you may experience some discomfort or even some guilt. If this is your experience, it will be important to remind yourself of three essential ideas:

1. Guilt is a powerful motivating force. It influences us to change our behaviour;

2. It would be easier for all of us if we could do things in retrospect. Unless we are professionally trained, none of us is taught how to help others with depression. We simply do the best that we can;

3. Use any painful or uncomfortable feelings you experience as an incentive to make positive changes in your life. Forgive yourself your past mistakes and start afresh from today.

TRAP 1

QUESTIONING

FOR MANY INDIVIDUALS WITH DEPRESSION,
SOME TYPES OF QUESTIONS MAY
EXACERBATE CYCLES OF RUMINATION.
BECAUSE OF THIS THEY NEED TO BE USED
WITH GREAT CAUTION.

HUSBAND: I really can't see how obtaining basic information is a problem. I also don't think it's reasonable to ask me to go through even a day without asking my wife questions!

THERAPIST: OK, I appreciate that this is a difficult concept. Just to clarify, I'm not talking about just any questions.

I'm talking specifically about questions that relate to your wife's depressed mood. I'll explain. Individuals with depression can spend a lot of time ruminating. In fact, on an average day they can sometimes spend hours at a time churning negative ideas over and over in their mind. They do this because they're trying to figure out why they feel the way they do, or they're trying to stop future problems occurring. All that their rumination tends to do, however, is to throw up ideas that create even more self-doubt and negative self-judgement, which makes their depressed mood worse.

The questions we ask are important, because if we approach someone who is experiencing depression and say things like, "Why are you feeling like this?" or, "What's the matter with you?", we're effectively mimicking part of the process that they already use to ruminate.

HUSBAND: I see what you're saying. But, if my wife is feeling depressed, haven't I got a right to know what's going on and what's causing it? After all, there are more people involved than just myself and my wife. If my wife's depressed it affects the whole family.

THERAPIST: OK, let's think about this in a different way. Tell me what you want to gain from knowing why your wife is depressed.

HUSBAND: Well if I know what's going on, I could help.

THERAPIST: How effective would you say your questions have been in helping your wife overcome her experience of depression?

HUSBAND: I don't know what you mean.

THERAPIST: What happens when you ask your wife questions like "Why are you feeling this way?"

HUSBAND: She says that she doesn't know.

THERAPIST: And what do you say then?

HUSBAND: I tell her that she should know.

THERAPIST: How do you feel when you
    try to get this information from her?

HUSBAND: Frustrated and helpless.

THERAPIST: So to recap, you ask
    questions because you have positive
    intentions and want to help, but what
    actually happens is that your wife
    closes down emotionally and you end
    up feeling frustrated and helpless.

HUSBAND: So what should I do then?

THERAPIST: Don't ask questions; instead
    acknowledge her feelings. Tell her it
    is OK for her to feel the way she does.
    When you do this, you'll be taking
    some of the pressure off her. The less
    time she spends ruminating on why

32

she feels the way she does, the
quicker her recovery will be.

Summary

Examples of questioning:

"Why are you feeling like this?"
"What's the matter with you?"
"What's wrong?"

Positive intention behind questioning.

We use questions such as those above to gather information so that we can help our loved ones feel better.

Result of questioning a depressed individual.

Individuals who are depressed will have already asked themselves the very same questions over and over again. Asking such questions instigates an internal problem-solving process that simply brings more negative self-opinion and self-judgement into their awareness. Your questions will provide further evidence that there is something wrong with them. This creates material for further rumination, which ultimately keeps their low mood in place. Unfortunately, when our loved one is depressed, such questions can also be perceived as judgemental or critical and will discourage dialogue.

Potential impact on us.

Our use of questioning could end up with us feeling helpless and low in respect of our inability to resolve the situation.

TRAP 2

RATIONALISING

RATIONALISING WITH INDIVIDUALS
ABOUT WHY THEY SHOULDN'T BE
FEELING DEPRESSED NEEDS TO BE
AVOIDED AT ALL COSTS.

MOTHER: But from what I understand
about Cognitive Behaviour Therapy,
isn't the whole idea that I should
give rational information to my son,
who's been suffering with depression
for years, so that he doesn't carry
on feeling the way that he does?

THERAPIST: So what information do you
give your son to help him rationalise?

MOTHER: I tell him that his family love him, and that I love him. I tell him that he's got a nice house, and that lots of people would be really happy if they had what he has.

THERAPIST: So how does your son react when you say these things?

MOTHER: He seems better … well for a little while.

THERAPIST: And how long does this last?

MOTHER: Not long.

THERAPIST: So what do you think he's gaining from your attempts to rationalise with him?

MOTHER: Not a lot, I guess. But why can't he see how lucky he is? It just doesn't make any sense to me.

THERAPIST: OK, let's put things into perspective. You rationalise with your son because you want to be helpful, because you want your son to realise that his life is much better than he thinks, and because there's no reason why he should feel depressed.

MOTHER: Exactly!

THERAPIST: But it doesn't work.

MOTHER: No.

THERAPIST: What would your reaction be if I told you that when you offer rational information to your son, he puts on a front to please you? That he then goes away from your conversation believing even more that there is something wrong or defective about himself for feeling the way that he does? And that this occurs as a direct result of your love and best attempts to be helpful?

MOTHER: I'd be mortified.

THERAPIST: Right. A key thing to be aware of is that rationalising doesn't work. It may help us feel better to state the obvious to others who are experiencing depression, because we don't like to see them suffering. But we need to ask ourselves, "How successful has this strategy been so far?"

SUMMARY

Examples of rationalising:

"You don't need to feel like this!"
"Look at what you have got. You've got a loving family, you've got a nice house."
"Lots of people would be grateful just to be in your position."

Positive intention behind rationalising.

We rationalise because we want to be helpful. We want our loved one to realise that life is much better than they think, and that there is no real reason why they should feel depressed.

Result.

Individuals who experience depression already know the facts about their situation. The message our loved one receives is that they are wrong in feeling the way they do. Feeling wrong about their feelings simply contributes further to their feelings of low mood, and fuels ideas that there is something defective about them.

Potential impact on us.

We may see our loved ones attempting to put on a positive front as they attempt to hide their feelings and please us. When this occurs we may end up feeling as though we're speaking to a veneer, without any sense of true connection.

TRAP 3

PROVIDING SOLUTIONS OR ADVICE

OFFERING SOLUTIONS AND ADVICE MAY
INITIALLY HELP US TO FEEL BETTER, BUT
OUR ADVICE IS UNLIKELY TO BE
FOLLOWED AND WE RUN THE RISK
OF BEING PERCEIVED AS CRITICAL
AND CONTROLLING.

FATHER: It seems from what you're
saying here that I should just
stand back and let my daughter
make the same mistakes over and
over again. Surely in anyone's eyes
that's neglectful or inconsiderate?

THERAPIST: OK, let's put this into

context. When your daughter is depressed, her concentration is poor, her memory is affected and many of the activities and tasks that she would have completed easily in the past now seem, to her, like climbing a mountain. So let's think about this for a minute. What impact do you think it would have on your daughter if I said things to her along the lines of:

"What you need to do is this … "
"If I were you I'd … " or
"Why don't you … ?"

FATHER: … I don't know. I've never really thought about it before … She'd probably feel criticised because she hadn't done these things herself.

But I'm her father and surely she knows that when I am saying these things, I'm thinking about her best interests. If she just did what I said, she'd be fine. I just can't understand why she won't listen to me.

THERAPIST: Just out of interest, how much of the time does your daughter follow the advice that you offer?

FATHER: Hardly ever.

THERAPIST: And how do you feel when you keep on offering all of this good advice, and yet she fails to follow it?

FATHER: Frustrated … powerless - to be honest I feel like I'm letting her down.

THERAPIST: So just to recap. You offer your daughter solutions on a regular basis because you love her, want to help her and want to be a good father. However, the very fact that you're telling her what to do leads to her feeling criticised and incapable. As a result, your daughter rarely – if ever – does what you say, and while all of this is going on you're feeling powerless and frustrated. So what do you make of that?

FATHER: You're making me feel like an idiot … when all I want to do is help my daughter.

THERAPIST: I appreciate that you feel that way, and it's not my intention for you to think of yourself as an idiot. The key point I'm raising here is that there's a huge gulf between what you want to happen and what's actually happening. You just need to be able to translate your positive intentions into results.

FATHER: I don't see how! I don't think anything will change this situation.

THERAPIST: OK, try this and see what happens.

Immediately, stop providing solutions and advice. You know it doesn't work because you've tried that already.

Instead, create a relaxed environment. Make it easier for your daughter to come to you to talk about her problems. When she does, listen to what she has to say without giving any suggestions or improvements. She'll be more likely to talk openly to you if she feels that you're accepting of her and non-judgmental. Most people prefer to work out their problems for themselves, and by listening you'll be giving her an opportunity to do that. Just wait, see what happens.

SUMMARY

Examples of providing solutions or advice:

"What you need to do is this … "
"If I were you I would … "
"Why don't you … ?"
"Have you thought about going to … ?"

The positive intention behind offering solutions and advice.

We offer solutions and advice to be helpful. The answers seem so clear, so why don't our loved ones see it?

Result.

Our loved ones already know they could do things differently, but when they're depressed they don't know what to do for the best, or how to do it. There's also a high risk of our being perceived as critical and controlling. This will instigate a thinking process whereby our loved one reflects on why they haven't done what you've suggested already. This provides further fuel for cycles of rumination, which keeps their low mood in place. Our loved one is also likely to feel misunderstood, further enhancing their feelings of failure, isolation and loneliness.

Potential impact on us.

We may end up feeling disempowered and frustrated, for although in our mind we will have offered good advice, we will also have to watch as our advice goes unheeded.

TRAP 4

DISAPPROVING OF OUR LOVED ONE'S LOW MOOD

DISAPPROVING OF OUR LOVED ONE'S
LOW MOOD CAN LEAD TO A PROGRESSIVE
DECLINE IN MOOD.

MOTHER: It seems from what you're
saying that I shouldn't disapprove
of my daughter spending all day in
bed, not working or doing anything,
while her father and myself spend
most of our time working to put
food on the table and pay the bills.
How is she going to learn about
responsibility? How is she going
to find out that these things don't
just happen by themselves? To be

56

honest, I'm just fed up with it!

THERAPIST: At present how do you
put these ideas across to her?

MOTHER: I tell her straight - just like I've
told you.

THERAPIST: In a frustrated, angry way?

MOTHER: Well ... yes. Otherwise, maybe
she'll think it's just all right to spend
all day in bed and then be up half of
the night.

THERAPIST: OK, and how often do you
tell her this just like you've told me?

MOTHER: Every time I see her.

THERAPIST: So tell me, how often do you
see your daughter?

MOTHER: Like I say, she gets up
at night and sleeps during the
day, so basically not too often,
Probably a couple of times a day.

THERAPIST: Have you ever wondered if
she might be avoiding you?

MOTHER: What do you mean?

THERAPIST: When your daughter feels the
way she does, how much do you think
that she feels approved of by you?

MOTHER: I don't disapprove of her.
I disapprove of her behaviour.

THERAPIST: And your daughter understands this difference?

MOTHER: I don't know.

THERAPIST: If you went somewhere where you felt that everyone else disapproved of your behaviour, what would you do?

MOTHER: I'd either change my behaviour, leave or I wouldn't go there in the first place!

THERAPIST: OK, so what would you think if I told you that your daughter spends a lot of time away from the rest of your family because she feels ashamed about her feelings? That she avoids you because

she feels disapproved of, leading
her to feel even more ashamed,
isolated, lonely and depressed?

MOTHER: I don't know... All that
I'm thinking right now is that I
must be a really bad mother.

THERAPIST: And that really hurts?

MOTHER: Yes.

THERAPIST: How would you feel if I said
to you that you actually feel this way
because you care so much? That
you've been doing what you've been
doing because part of you hopes
that, if you show sufficient disapproval, your daughter will wake
up one day and decide that she is

no longer going to be depressed?

MOTHER: If I'm really honest with
myself, that's actually what I want.

THERAPIST: But we also know that you've
tried disapproval enough times to
understand that it doesn't work,
and it is unlikely to ever work.

MOTHER: So what do I do?

THERAPIST: A fundamental concept
to consider here is that fighting
low mood doesn't work. Nor will
any other strategy that falls into
this category, such as struggling
with it or refusing to accept it.
These types of strategies will
simply lead your daughter to

61

become even more "stuck", which no doubt will feel like a desperate and despairing place for her.

MOTHER: But that's the last thing I would want for her.

THERAPIST: I know, so now's the time to try something new. Tell your daughter it's OK for her to feel the way that she does. You may feel uncomfortable with this because our natural inclination is to avoid pain. Few of us stop and try such a radical strategy as approaching and accepting low mood. Approach your daughter and – even if she pushes you away – let her know that you will be there for her if she decides she wants to talk. Remind her that from this point on you're there to help, not to control.

SUMMARY

Examples of disapproval:

Shouting.
Losing our temper.
Using behavioural gestures such as rolling our
eyes or shaking our head.

Positive intention behind disapproval.

When we show disapproval, our intention is to
help our loved one understand that depression is
bad for them. We think that if we show enough
disapproval, then they might simply stop feeling
the way that they do, or that their depressed mood
might simply go away.

Result.

Many individuals who experience depression have
learnt (often in their childhood) that their self-

worth is conditional on the approval that they get from others. Our behaviour may lead them to try not to be depressed or to try to control their low mood. These types of behaviour can lead to them feeling progressively lower. Our loved one may also try to hide their low mood from us, leaving them feeling even more isolated, embarrassed and ashamed about their feelings.

Potential impact on us.

We are more likely to continue feeling frustrated, and after reflection we may also experience shame and guilt about our own behaviour.

TRAP 5

AVOIDING OUR LOVED ONE'S LOW MOOD

AVOIDING OUR LOVED ONE'S LOW MOOD
SIMPLY REINFORCES THEIR BELIEFS ABOUT
BEING WORTHLESS. WE MAY ALSO BEGIN
TO FEEL INCREASINGLY HELPLESS ABOUT
HOW WE CAN RESOLVE THE SITUATION.

PARTNER: But, with the case of my
    partner, Brian … he's so moody. I
    believe that he's actually better off
    spending more time by himself.

THERAPIST: And you think this way
    because … ?

PARTNER: Well, everything I do seems to

irritate him. I'm sure that if I spent more time with him, he'd just feel even worse.

THERAPIST: So what do you do to give Brian more time to himself?

PARTNER: If any extra shifts come up at work, I usually volunteer for them. It's not like I spend a lot of time away with friends, having fun or anything like that.

THERAPIST: What conclusions do you think Brian comes to about why you are spending more time at work?

PARTNER: He thinks I'm trying to be away from him.

THERAPIST: What do you think Brian thinks to himself when he spends more time on his own?

PARTNER: I don't know … I haven't thought about it … He's not worth spending time around, maybe – but you've got to understand! You'd have to see it for yourself! For me it's a no-win situation.

THERAPIST: So how long has this been going on for?

PARTNER: About 12 months.

THERAPIST: How did you feel about Brian before he became depressed?

PARTNER: He was one of the first people

that I met that I felt I could truly
love, and I really thought that this
was the man that I'd grow old with.

THERAPIST: What do you see happening
   if things keep going the way that
   they are?

PARTNER: I don't know … I don't want to
   think about it. It's too frightening.

THERAPIST: It may help if we just go
   there for a minute. What do you
   think might happen?

PARTNER: If I'm honest, I think my love
   for him is dying and I worry about
   the relationship lasting.

THERAPIST: Does Brian know about this?

PARTNER: No, we don't talk about it.

THERAPIST: OK, let's recap. When you met Brian he was one of the first people that you felt you could truly love. Now that he's become depressed, you've been spending more and more time away from him. … to help him. However, the more time he spends on his own, the more worthless he feels and things still haven't got any better. In fact, they've got worse and it's got to the point where you are not sure about your feelings for him anymore. On top of this, you also have doubts about the relationship lasting.

PARTNER: What am I supposed to do?

THERAPIST: The first thing to recognise is that avoiding the problem isn't working. In fact, it's making it worse. What you will need to do is the opposite. Approach the problem and tolerate your own feelings of discomfort around his irritation.

PARTNER: So how do I do that?

THERAPIST: Remind yourself that you are not responsible for his irritation. It's not your job to keep him happy. Instead, let him know that it's OK for him to feel the way that he does. He already feels really bad about himself and probably has some of the same worries about the relationship that you have. When you spend more time around him, he is less likely to think that your past avoidance behaviour means something negative about him. This will take some of the pressure off and help his recovery.

SUMMARY

Examples of avoiding low mood:

Spending more time at work and away from
our loved one.
Creating reasons why we need to be somewhere
else.

Positive intention behind avoiding low mood.

Often, when we avoid our loved ones low mood,
we are not even aware that we are doing it. But
sometimes we avoid them consciously because
we feel we cannot do anything to change the
situation. We justify to ourselves why it is best to
have less contact. Alternatively, we think that if
maybe we spend more time around our loved one
when they are low, we are encouraging their low
mood in some way and, if we avoid it, it will go
away by itself.

Result.

Individuals who experience depression are likely
to interpret our behaviour as meaning something
negative, and then use this as evidence to support
their beliefs of low worth, not being good enough
or insignificant etc. From a behavioural point of
view, they are also likely to be spending more
time on their own, feeling lonely or isolated.

Potential impact on us.

We may end up feeling that we are drifting
further and further apart from them and more
helpless about resolving the situation.

TRAP 6

CRITICISING OUR LOVED ONE FOR EXPERIENCING DEPRESSION

MANY PEOPLE DO NOT UNDERSTAND
THAT WHEN WE ARE CRITICAL, IT'S
BECAUSE WE CARE. HOWEVER, BEING
CRITICAL TO SOMEONE WHO IS DEPRESSED
WILL SIMPLY RE-INFORCE THEIR ALREADY
NEGATIVE SELF-VIEW.

FATHER: You could be the best psychologist or therapist in the land for all I know, but unless you've been in the position I've been in, you could never appreciate just how hard it is for me to watch a grown man in his thirties make a complete mess of his life, and not comment on it.

THERAPIST: Think of all of the other people that you come into contact with. Is there any difference between them and your son?

FATHER: Well, with no disrespect to other people, I care more deeply about my son.

THERAPIST: Does he know that you feel this way about him when you try to help him by being critical?

FATHER: He must do. Of course I don't tell him. I'm sure he knows how I feel about him.

THERAPIST: So what kind of things do you say to him?

FATHER: I tell him that now that he's in his thirties he should already be established. He should have sorted the mess that he's got himself into and made something of himself a long time ago.

THERAPIST: So how does he react when you tell him this?

FATHER: I don't know really. He doesn't seem to take anything much that I say on board.

THERAPIST: How do you react when he doesn't listen to you?

FATHER: I don't know. I keep trying to tell him and I just hope that a little bit sinks in.

THERAPIST: So how much do you think has sunk in so far?

FATHER: I don't think anything has sunk in.

THERAPIST: How long have you been trying to help him like this?

FATHER: I don't know, I'd say about 15, maybe 20 years.

THERAPIST: How do you feel when, despite your best efforts over so much time, nothing changes?

FATHER: I would disown him if I could, but he's my son and so I could never do that.

THERAPIST: So how do you think your
    son feels about nothing changing?

FATHER: I don't know.

THERAPIST: OK, let's think about this in
    another way. What do you think your
    son thinks about himself not being
    established by now?

FATHER: I'd guess that he's disappointed
    in himself.

THERAPIST: Let's recap then, because
    I want to make sure I've got this
    right. You're critical to your son
    because you care about his future.
    And, in fact, you're more critical
    to your son than you are to others
    because you care so much about

him. You keep trying to tell your son to change, but despite saying the same things to him for over 15 years it still hasn't worked.

As well as this, we know that your son has heard this information for over 15 years, and now probably uses that information to tell himself off for not being how he thinks he should be. When he's depressed, the thought about how much you love him probably doesn't come into his mind and he probably feels like a big disappointment to you. So how does this help him take charge of his life?

FATHER: If you think you could do a better job, be my guest. At this point I feel like throwing in the towel.

THERAPIST: OK, I appreciate this isn't easy – but you're still the best person for this job. We just need to think about things in a different way. In what you say to your son, you can make much more impact on him than most other people in his life. All we are identifying here are some basic facts: that the love and positive intentions that you have for your son are not being converted into the results that you want.

FATHER: You're the expert, what do you suggest then?

THERAPIST: Initially, this is likely to feel very strange to you, because it's different to what you're used to. What I recommend is that you go to your son at the earliest opportunity and be honest with him. He's not a mind reader, so tell him how you really feel about him. Tell him about all the things that you like about him and apologise for being critical of him over the years. Take ownership of the fact that you have probably contributed in some way to how he is feeling about himself. Tell him that his feelings are normal. As I have already said, this will feel unusual and difficult at first, and for many of us it is far easier to carry on using unproductive strategies because they're what we're used to.

If you make these positive changes I predict that you will achieve highly noticeable results.

SUMMARY

Examples of criticism:

"You're weak ... pathetic,"
"Are you going to stay in your room for ever?"
"It's not normal to behave this way!"
"Why don't you just get over it?"
"I can't understand what's wrong with you."

Positive intention behind criticism.

When we are critical to our loved ones, we want them to see the error of their ways and to decide to be different and to change their behaviour. We are critical because we care, and we can often be more critical with people we love the most.

Result.

Our loved ones, when experiencing depression, may not realise that our reaction to them is driven by our own fear, anxiety, or sense of responsibility for their well-being.

Individuals who are susceptible to depression already tend to be highly self-critical, and often are far more critical about themselves than we are. Our criticisms will simply be used to confirm or supply further evidence for the negative thoughts they've already had about themselves.

Potential impact on us.

Our criticisms are unlikely to improve the situation for our loved ones. As well as this we may end up feeling powerless, ashamed, frustrated and guilty.

TRAP 7

TEACHING

BE CAREFUL ABOUT TRYING TO TEACH
SOMEONE WHO IS DEPRESSED ABOUT HOW
THEIR LOW MOOD IMPACTS ON OTHERS,
AS THIS IS LIKELY TO REINFORCE THEIR
BELIEFS ABOUT BEING BAD
AND WORTHLESS.

MOTHER: So how else am I going to encourage my daughter to stop the self-
destructive behaviours that she seems
to think it's a good idea to keep
engaging in? How is she ever going
to be able to live with others if no one
tells her what she is doing wrong?

THERAPIST: So what kinds of things do you say to her?

MOTHER: Basically, I ask her if she has ever considered the effect that her behaviour has on the rest of us, or how she thinks I feel when she behaves the way he does.

THERAPIST: So how does she react to your questions and statements?

MOTHER: She doesn't answer. Walks off, bangs doors and, to all intents and purposes, ignores me.

THERAPIST: How do you think she feels when she does this?

MOTHER: I don't really know … as I said,

she walks off. Maybe she doesn't like what she's hearing and what I'm saying is registering with her at some level.

THERAPIST: So what do you think she's registering to herself when she is banging doors and walking off?

MOTHER: Guilt about her behaviour, I expect.

THERAPIST: So how do you think this will help her with this depression?

MOTHER: I don't know – but I can't see how things could get much worse.

THERAPIST: What would you think if I said to you that, like many other individuals who experience depression, your daughter already believes that she needs to please others? That she already feels ashamed and guilty about being depressed?

MOTHER: I can't really see it – well, not at home any way.

THERAPIST: OK, let's think about this in a different way. What's your daughter like when she's not depressed?

MOTHER: She's always doing things to help other people. She's polite, well meaning and considerate.

THERAPIST: So how do you think she feels when, because of her depression, she can't be like she normally is?

MOTHER: I don't know … I haven't thought about it this way before. I suppose she must feel guilty.

THERAPIST: OK, let's recap. Your daughter hears you suggesting that she should go back to pleasing others and thinking of other people's needs, just like before. We know that physically she can't do this when she is depressed and she hears a message from you telling her that she should push down her own painful feelings and think about others.

MOTHER: You've put it in a way that I haven't thought about before … Actually, what I'm doing doesn't sound too helpful does it?

THERAPIST: As parents, all we can do is the best we can, and inevitably from time to time we all make mistakes. But there is good news. At this stage, all of us have an opportunity to apologise for our mistakes and start again. It is important that you reinforce to your daughter that it is completely OK for her to feel the way that she does. Show her through your behaviour that her feelings are just as important as everybody else's in the world. This will decrease her vulnerability to further periods of depression.

Summary

Examples of teaching:

"Don't you realise how you make me feel when you do this?"
"Have you considered the effect your behaviour has on the rest of us?"

Positive intention behind teaching.

When we attempt to teach, we are trying to be helpful. We want our loved ones to understand that their symptoms of depression can have an impact on others. Our aim is to help our loved one to take responsibility for the way that they are feeling and to help them make positive changes for themselves.

Result.

Our loved ones will be more likely to think

that they are causing harm to others because of the way that they feel. Individuals who are susceptible to depression already feel guilty and ashamed when they feel low, and our comments will simply reinforce these feelings. Individuals who experience depression often have a tendency to want to please others, and our comments will reinforce within them the idea that other people's feelings are more important than theirs. Teaching may also send a subtle message to our loved one that their feelings are unbearable, unacceptable, or faulty in some way.

Potential impact on us.

We are likely to feel ashamed and guilty as we see how our loved one reacts to our comments. We will also have to watch as they become angry or even more withdrawn.

TRAP 8

OVERPROTECTION

OVERPROTECTION OF OUR LOVED ONE
WHEN THEY ARE LOW WILL SIMPLY
MAKE THEM FEEL MORE FRAGILE,
AND MUST BE AVOIDED

HUSBAND: I hear what you're saying
but I can't agree with you. My
real concern is that I am actually
not doing enough to protect
my wife, because she's getting
worse rather than better.

THERAPIST: So what's been happening?

HUSBAND: My wife was admitted to

hospital a few years back and
she hated it. After they sectioned
her, we both felt that I'd let her
down. I would hate for her ever
to go back to that place.

THERAPIST: So what do you do now to
help her?

HUSBAND: Well, I do everything around
the house, because if she sees a messy
house she thinks it's her fault. I
screen all telephone calls for her,
because she tends to get worn out
after she speaks to some of her
friends. Sometimes I stop our teenage
children bringing their friends home
because my wife gets upset by all
their noise and shouting.

THERAPIST: So what does your wife think about this?

HUSBAND: I don't know. I try not to tell her too much because it could make her feel worse.

THERAPIST: So what kinds of things do you and the children tell her?

HUSBAND: I don't know … I just keep the conversation short and I stop the children telling her anything that might worry her.

THERAPIST: Does she know that you stop the children telling her things?

HUSBAND: I think so, because she's heard me stopping them on a few occasions.

THERAPIST: So how does your wife react to this?

HUSBAND: I don't know – she just seems to start crying. Like I said it makes her worse.

THERAPIST: How long has this been going on for?

HUSBAND: About six months.

THERAPIST: What do you think your wife thinks about herself, with you and your children doing these things to protect her?

HUSBAND: I don't know. Like I said, that's not a conversation that I'd have with my wife.

THERAPIST: OK. Let's guess instead!

HUSBAND: This is hard … I don't know
… What do you want me to say?

THERAPIST: Let's try this in a different
way. For a few minutes put yourself
in your wife's place, thinking and
feeling the way that she does. If your
husband and your children were
doing various things to protect you,
how would you feel?

HUSBAND: OK … I would hate it – but
then again I'm not my wife, am I?

THERAPIST: So, what would you hate?

HUSBAND: Well I'd feel weak, and with
everyone doing things for me, I'd

think that it really was true that …

THERAPIST: It was really true that … ?

HUSBAND: That I'm incapable of looking after myself.

THERAPIST: How would your wife feel about that?

HUSBAND: Well, she'd be frightened about feeling worse and ending up in hospital like last time … but at the same time it's kind of strange, because I think I'd be relieved at the same time.

THERAPIST: OK. Let's recap. Your wife's been experiencing depression for six months and during this time you've done everything that you can to protect her from feeling bad, but it's still not working – in fact, it's getting worse. The more you do things for her, the more incapable she feels about herself. While this is going on you're feeling more and more anxious about your wife deteriorating further. It's come to the point where part of you would feel relieved if she were sectioned again. So what would happen if you tried to protect her even more?

HUSBAND: Logically … her depression will get worse … but I don't know what else to do.

THERAPIST: OK, try this. Stop protecting her. Encourage her to carry out activities where results can be achieved very quickly with little effort, such as completing short walks, and eating small snacks. Remind her that it is normal to feel slowed up and to have poor concentration and memory. While acknowledging that it's OK for her to feel depressed, tell her about her past achievements. Tell her how much you and your children love her. Remind yourself that there is little to lose by trying out a new approach. Be curious and see what happens.

Summary

Examples of overprotection:

Helping our loved one by taking over tasks that they would normally carry out.
Telling others how to behave towards them, e.g. "Don't upset your mother, brother, father" "Watch what you're saying please".

Positive intention behind overprotection.

To protect our loved one from potential further low mood.

Result.

When we overprotect, we demonstrate to our loved one that we think that they are not capable of looking after themselves. This is likely to exacerbate their feelings of low self-worth, and increase their avoidance, which will contribute to them experiencing continued depression. Their problems will seem even more significant if they perceive that we are helping them to avoid things. Overprotection is also likely to project feelings of fragility and helplessness onto our loved one.

Potential impact on us.

We may end up feeling increasingly anxious as our attempts to protect our loved one result in little improvement. Confusion and resentment may also set in, as the more we are doing to "help" our loved one, the more disabled and withdrawn they appear to become.

CONCLUSION

CONSIDER CHANGING YOUR BEHAVIOUR
OR, IF YOU CANNOT CHANGE YOUR
BEHAVIOUR, CONSIDER ALTERING YOUR
PERCEPTION OF YOUR SITUATION.
EITHER WAY – TAKE ACTION!

What do I do if I fall into the traps?

Falling into any of the Traps 1–8 indicates that a change of approach is required. When we use the same approach over and over again, especially when we know that it has never worked, we need to ask ourselves, "What will happen if I keep trying this?" Think of a fly trying over and over again to get through a pane of glass. Ask yourself "Could this apply to my behaviour?"

CHANNEL YOUR POSITIVE INTENTIONS
INTO BEHAVIOURS THAT WORK.

You can make a big difference.

The fact that you are reading this book shows that
you already have high levels of positive intention.
So let's turn this intention into results that work.
Read the ideas covered in the next few pages and
understand them. Discussing them with your
loved one will be helpful.

Fighting low mood does not work!

The process of fighting depression is not unlike
the childhood story of the Sun and the Wind.
The Wind approaches the Sun and suggests a

competition to see which of them is the more powerful. The Wind points out a man standing below wearing a coat, and suggests that the strongest should surely be able to get the man to remove his coat. The Wind tries first, but the harder it blows the more the man clings onto his coat. The Wind eventually withdraws, exhausted, thinking that it will be impossible for the Sun to get the man to remove his coat. The Sun then says "I'll try", and simply does nothing but shine, easily and effortlessly. Of course, to the Wind's astonishment the man removes his coat.

The message is simple: sometimes when we try too hard we can make our situation worse.

So what can we do?

The first issue that we will need to address is how we react to our own painful feelings. To watch someone we love suffering feels incredibly painful and can provoke fear in us. Our natural inclination when we experience pain is to try to get rid of it. This presents a dilemma, because

in trying to get rid of our pain, we can resort
to using strategies that result in our loved one's
situation becoming worse, as shown in Traps 1—8.

**If we learn how to respond well to our own
feelings, we can help our loved one respond
well to theirs.**

The first step we need to take is to improve
awareness of our own feelings. In our companion
book "Think about your thinking to stop
depression" there are a number of strategies that
detail how to work with your feelings. When we
have decided it is OK for us to feel the way we do,
we will then feel under less pressure to resolve
our loved one's situation. As a result of this, any
tension that we may feel will begin to lift. This
is a very important strategy for us to master,
because when we feel under less pressure, the
pressure will also lift from our loved ones.

WHAT TO DO AND SAY.

Tell your loved one that it is OK for him or her to feel the way they do.

Many of us feel that if we allow pain to be there, in this case the pain of low mood, it will get worse, and spiral out of control. We do not stop to think about trying such a radical strategy as approaching it. Try out the ideas covered in this section and see what occurs. Do your expectations match what actually happens?

Help our loved one come to us.

As identified in the Traps section of this book, attempting to speed up the process of our loved one's movement out of a depressed state, by trying too hard, can have negative results.

Instead we will need to concentrate on creating a relaxed and more accepting atmosphere, so that our loved one will be more likely to turn to us to talk about what is troubling them. Individuals vulnerable to becoming depressed are much more likely to talk openly to others who they believe will be accepting and non-judgemental of them.

Key issues to be aware of when our loved one comes to us.

We will need to listen without providing solutions and explain to our loved one that it is really OK for them to feel the way they do. We can tell our loved one that anyone who has similar problems or similar thoughts would feel the same way they do. If our loved one comes up with their own solutions, we need to encourage them without suggesting any improvements that might come to our minds.

We will also need to bear in mind that if we fall into any of the traps mentioned earlier, that any productive or helpful conversation could come to a very speedy end.

How to respond to thinking errors that many individuals with depression have.

Individuals who are vulnerable to becoming depressed are likely to think in an "all or nothing way" when they are experiencing depression. They may even say things such as "it is always going to be this way" "... all of the time ..." "nothing ever works out ... " and we rarely hear the words "sometimes" or "occasionally". It is important here that we do not come up with alternative evidence or argue against their position, as this can have the unfortunate consequence of keeping rigid thinking styles in place. Instead we will need to say things such as "I know that you feel this way right now. Even though you don't believe it right now, things will change, things will get better".

Advice to parents who have depressed adult offspring.

How to help our children when they have low mood or if they are experiencing depression.

Watching our children suffer can induce considerable fear in us. The press frequently publish reports about individuals who have taken their own lives. There is no more awful a thought for parents than their children killing themselves. Many of us take action (i.e., helping our children) to decrease our fear – often falling into the traps already outlined. When we take this type of action we can often be perceived as controlling by our children, which ultimately can contribute to and exacerbate their problems.

As parents we are more likely to fall into traps than any other group of people who come into contact with individuals experiencing depression. With two concerned parents trying to help there is an even greater chance for traps to be activated. There can also be other problematic knock-on effects when siblings become involved.

As a parent, a major issue that we have to deal with is responsibility, and that somehow and in some way, we are responsible for how our child is feeling. This can result in us trying too hard to help our child.

We are naturally inclined to want to question our children about how and why they are feeling the way they are. This is because we want to help them resolve their difficulties. Naturally, such questions can be particularly difficult for young people to address.

So a general rule of thumb to bear in mind is to avoid at all costs falling into Traps 1–8.

Here are examples of what you can do.

Ask no questions (e.g., "What's wrong?" "What's the matter?"). Instead tell your son or daughter that if they want someone to talk to, that you will be there for them.

Concentrate on creating an environment that makes it easier for them to approach you.

Be non-judgemental and use praise.

Instead of trying to rationalise their feelings away, let them know that it is OK to feel the way that they do. If they are young adults, explain to them that the way they feel (while unpleasant) is normal and is often part of growing up.

Offer no solutions unless they are asked for.

If they are young adults, tell them that low feelings although unpleasant, are something that our body produces to help us.

Approach your child, even if they push you away.

Let them know that you are there for them.

Praise them for all of their good points and tell them how much you love them.

View yourself as being there to help, not to control.

Let your child know that their feelings are accepted.

As parents we can have much more influence than we realise.

Sometimes we don't tell our children how much we love them. Sometimes we don't apologise for things that we have done wrong, or for mistakes we have made in the past. Letting our children know that we have made errors is very important, as many children often blame themselves needlessly for things that were not their fault.

It is important that we do not seek forgiveness as our child may well try to minimise issues to protect us and they may say things such as "don't worry about it, it was nothing".

Many things that cause pain are not forgotten, even if they happened several years, even decades, before. It is never too late to say sorry.

How do we react to our feelings when our children tell us things about ourselves that we don't want to hear?

It is important to listen to our children and to let them speak. Sometimes they will say things that may be painful to hear, and when this occurs it is easy to get drawn into a defensive position. If this occurs, we need to encourage ourselves to acknowledge our own feelings and resist the urge to defend ourselves. If we do this, we will be carrying out excellent parenting behaviour. We will be showing our child how to accept responsibility by direct modelling and demonstration. In this case, actions definitely speak louder than words!

Even though we love our children, we need to

remind ourselves that they cannot read our minds.

If we find it hard to express ourselves to our children, it can be very helpful to write them a letter telling them all the things that we like and love about them, and letting them know how we feel about them. We will need to choose our compliments very carefully, without criticism and – very importantly – without trying to teach.

If our child has made mistakes, which they regret, we can remind them how useful it is to make mistakes as this is how we all grow and develop.

Finally, as parents we are the most important role models in our children's lives. We must not under any circumstances underestimate how important we are to them.

ADVICE TO PARTNERS OF THOSE WHO ARE EXPERIENCING LOW MOOD OR DEPRESSION.

If our partner is suffering with depression, then there is little we can do to avoid it. It will impact on us as well.

Most people who are depressed find reading difficult. You can increase their motivation by doing things with them such as reading this book. People who are vulnerable to depression feel less alone if their partners take part in their recovery. Consider it a joint project!

The topics covered in this book's companion "Think about your thinking to stop depression" may not make sense to those who have never been depressed, so reading and understanding how the methods work will be very useful.

For many individuals who experience depression there is a shift in their libido. Anti-depressants can also have a negative impact on sexual interest.

If our partner does not want to have sex, we need to remind ourselves that it does not necessarily mean anything about us. If we believe that our partner's lack of interest in sex is about us, then we may feel rejected and engage in behaviours that will not help our partner's mood.

Depression can also affect our partner's ability to complete usual activities that would have previously been no problem. As suggested in the traps section, showing disapproval of their behaviour is unlikely to help lift them out of a depressed state.

Specific behaviours to avoid if our partner is experiencing depression.

- Flirting with other individuals

- Threatening to leave our partner
- Comparing our partner to previous partners
- Looking upon our partner as lazy and selfish
- Being cross or angry with their mood
- Keeping their experience of depression a big secret
- Dropping our own interests and hobbies

Important things that we can do.

Let them know that it's OK for them to feel the way that they do.

If children are involved, tell them what an important figure they are in their children's lives.

Tell them all the things that you love and appreciate about them and feel grateful for about them.

Encourage and support them to carry out activities where results can be achieved very quickly with little effort e.g., short walks, eating small amounts, being around others, and having short conversations.

Acknowledge their achievements, making it clear that you know that they might not see things as achievements because these were all things they could do before without much effort. A major problem that keeps people depressed is focussing on what they used to do and then telling themselves off for not being able to do it when they are experiencing depression. All this tends to do is to keep them stuck.

Tell them that you understand they are not where they want to be yet, but that it's about getting there bit by bit.

Remind them of the question –
"How do you eat an elephant?"
Answer – "One bite at a time"

Remind them about how common depression is, that it is normal, and what is more important is how it is reacted to.

When our partner is depressed, it is important to be tactile. But, as already mentioned, their libido is likely to be depressed as well. So when we are being tactile with our partner we need to touch them in a non-sexual way (e.g., touching their face, feet, arms, back, hair etc). They need to be free from any illusion that we might want them to "perform" sexually.

If, as a partner, you feel angry, irritated or resentful about following any of the above advice, then it may be that your relationship with your loved one is a factor in their symptoms of depression. It is not unusual for this to occur. However, it is important to be aware of it and to acknowledge it as a problem in its own right, and then take steps to address it together.

INDEX

INDEX

...THERE NOW FOLLOWS A SHORT EXTRACT FROM THE FOLLOWING TITLE...

THINK ABOUT YOUR THINKING TO STOP DEPRESSION

A FAST SIMPLE SYSTEM TO RELIEVE DISTRESS

Dr Nicola Ridgeway, ClinPsyD
Dr James Manning, ClinPsyD

Published by The West Suffolk CBT Service Limited
Registered office: Angel Corner, 8 Angel Hill,
Bury St Edmunds, Suffolk, IP33 1UZ

INTRODUCTION

This book has been written to help you break unhelpful patterns of thinking. Patterns that can lead to depression.

The book is divided into 18 sessions, each of which, on average, will take no more than five minutes to read. Each session begins with a summary of its essential theme. This is then explored, in dialogue, between a Cognitive Behaviour Therapist and a client. Reflection boxes are scattered throughout the book to draw your attention to ideas of particular importance.

Pratical exercises and additional information, about each session, can be gained via our manual "Think about your thinking – Cognitive Behaviour Therapy Programme for Depression."

SESSION 1

THE PARADOX OF ACCEPTANCE

ACCEPTING YOUR FEELINGS IS ESSENTIAL
TO STOP DETERIORATION IN YOUR MOOD.

CLIENT: But that makes absolutely no
sense to me at all. Why would I want
to accept that I'm feeling this way,
when all I really want is for these
feelings to go away?

THERAPIST: Well, just ask yourself, has
trying to get rid of your feelings
worked so far?

CLIENT: I guess not!

THERAPIST: I'll explain what I mean. All emotions have a function, even those that don't feel nice (such as guilt, shame, disgust, and sadness) and we have evolved to have *all* of our feelings. What impact would there be on society if nobody ever processed painful feelings? Feeling low is often connected to a process of loss, whether this is a physical loss, or a loss of something that had the potential to happen. What would life be like if nobody experienced loss? Indeed, what would life be like if nobody experienced guilt when they had actually done something wrong? Where would the motivation for people to make positive changes come from?

The majority of us experience low mood for valid reasons. However, for many of us the triggers are not immediately clear. I'll explain more thoroughly why this occurs in future sessions. What I'm inviting you to consider right now though is that whatever route we take to find the triggers for our moods, we will ultimately find a good and logical reason for why we have been feeling the way we have.

CLIENT: Erm? I wish it were that easy!

THERAPIST: OK. Let me put it another way. What I'm inviting you to do is quite simply to leap ahead to that point where you have found the trigger for your low mood state and welcome your low mood. I say this because if we don't welcome our low mood, it's likely that we will receive multiple low mood messages that arrive with increasing strength, until the message is eventually heard. This will ultimately make us feel worse.

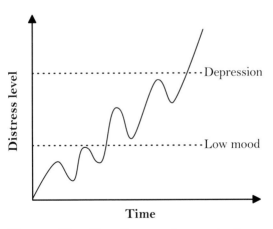

Figure 1. The effect of suppressing or rejecting painful feelings

CLIENT: So why does this happen?

THERAPIST: Because feelings are basic survival mechanisms that are very intent on getting their message through to us. Their purpose is to help us survive, so if we reject them they may subside in the short term, but will return later with increased strength. Basically, our feelings do this because they are trying to keep us safe, whether that is from physical threat – for example, being physically harmed – or from psychological threat – for example, being rejected or isolated from our familiar social group.

CLIENT: I mean no disrespect by this, but what you're saying makes absolutely no sense to me at all! You're saying that my feelings are trying to help me and I need to accept them, but I feel like they're trying to harm me!

THERAPIST: OK! I understand that … and, to be honest, if it made sense most people would already have found out about acceptance and they would be trying it, wouldn't they? So, given the number of people in our society who have depression, how many of these individuals are telling themselves that it's OK to feel the way that they do?

CLIENT: Not many, I suppose.

THERAPIST: That's right! So part of our solution lies here. When we accept our feelings, we consciously let our brains know that we have received the low mood message. This removes the necessity for the brain to continue sending low mood messages with increasing strength, and reduces the risk of our mood deteriorating. So what could you do to see if this works for you?

CLIENT: I suppose I could try your idea.

THERAPIST: Good for you!

REFLECTION

If we interpret something in our environment as harmful or dangerous in some way, then we come to the realisation that there is potential for pain. This can occur within both our:

- External environment (e.g. an event or the action of another individual);
- Internal environment (i.e. feelings, thoughts, physical sensations).

We naturally like to avoid pain or stop pain from continuing. So let's use the example of feeling low. There is nothing pleasurable about feeling low. So if we acknowledge and label our low feeling for what it is, it immediately stops the brain from (a) trying to work out why the low feeling is there and (b) trying to stop the low feeling from being there.

...This concludes the short extract, more information about this title can be found at http://www.westsuffolkcbt.com

THINK ABOUT YOUR THINKING TO STOP DEPRESSION. A FAST SIMPLE SYSTEM TO RELIEVE DISTRESS

A depressed state can have a very negative impact on the way that we process information. This can hamper our ability to step out of painful cycles of thoughts, feelings and behaviours that ultimately lead to prolonged suffering.

Reading when we are depressed can feel like a highly effortful process. This highly regarded book has been especially designed to be discrete, portable and to allow helpful information to be absorbed when concentration is poor.

Dr Nicola Ridgeway, ClinPsyD
Dr James Manning, ClinPsyD

Published by The West Suffolk CBT Service Limited
Registered office: Angel Corner, 8 Angel Hill,
Bury St Edmunds, Suffolk, IP33 1UZ

Price £9.95

THINK ABOUT YOUR THINKING - COGNITIVE BEHAVIOUR THERAPY PROGRAMME FOR DEPRESSION

If you found "Think about your thinking to stop depression" helpful, this manualised programme will take you to the next level.

Sessions within "Think about your thinking" are elaborated with exercises, worksheets and novel self-reflection exercises.

Dr Nicola Ridgeway, ClinPsyD
Dr James Manning, ClinPsyD

Published by The West Suffolk CBT Service Limited
Registered office: Angel Corner, 8 Angel Hill,
Bury St Edmunds, Suffolk, IP33 1UZ

Price £59.95